T0065369

ABCs
OF
LEADERSHIP
LEADERSHIP GUIDING PRINCIPLES

Henrietta N. Ukwu MD

authorHOUSE®

AuthorHouse™
1663 Liberty Drive
Bloomington, IN 47403
www.authorhouse.com
Phone: 833-262-8899

Published by AuthorHouse 11/17/2020

ISBN: 978-1-6655-0763-9 (sc)
ISBN: 978-1-6655-0762-2 (hc)
ISBN: 978-1-6655-0761-5 (e)

Library of Congress Control Number: 2020922506

Print information available on the last page.

Developing leadership potential is essential for making one's mark on the world. However, busy professionals do not always have time for leadership retreats or to read extensively about leadership. Even when they manage to attend retreats or read books, the topics covered are often narrow, offering only partial insight into how to hone leadership skills. To address these problems, this short book provides a quick yet comprehensive treatment of leadership, including practical tips that readers can use to make a difference in their lives and workplaces today. By working their way through the alphabet letter by letter, readers can explore all the traits and skills needed to become a leader and advance the causes that are important to them.

The structure of this book emerged over many decades of experience. While serving in corporate and community leadership roles, I realized that I could capture the description of leadership using the alphabet. Just as the alphabet forms the backbone of written language, so leadership provides the bedrock for effective and efficient organizations of all sorts. In addition, like the alphabet, the elements of leadership, from concept to application, are elegant in their simplicity. In moving through the alphabet, it is interesting to see how leadership-related words are so interconnected, weaving into one another effortlessly!

I hope that every reader will recognize and nurture the leader that lies within themself. Every day, we see news of great people leading nations, corporations, churches, communities, initiatives, and movements. We emulate their attributes and leadership styles and wonder if we, too, could rise to the occasion. This book's central message is that yes, each of us can, in our own way. However, we must first recognize that we are all both leaders and followers, and we must endeavor to fill both roles as best we can. As entrepreneur Malcolm Forbes said, "No one is a leader if there are no followers." Indeed, leaders are only as strong as their followers (or teams) make them. Conversely, leaders drive the culture, motivation, and outcomes of the teams they lead. Therefore, this book emphasizes team dynamics and outcomes as an essential component of leadership, placing a strong focus on relationships.

Leadership has many definitions, descriptions, theories, and categorizations, but all incorporate an appreciation of human attributes, behaviors, and characters: the **ABCs** of leadership. How do leaders harness this appreciation to motivate individuals to commit to a cause and achieve a goal together? By being **a**ppealing, **b**old, and **c**harismatic. Some individuals are deemed "born leaders," exhibiting from birth the strength of character that breeds affection and commands respect. When they speak, people listen and believe what they say. These individuals can seemingly effortlessly espouse a vision, galvanize a following, and drive success. However, even those of us who are not "born leaders" can *become* leaders by refining their skills through a variety of means: tools, training, effective leadership behavior modeling, coaching, mentoring, and receiving and addressing constructive feedback. That's where this book comes in. It is a window into the traits and practices needed to cultivate the leader within each of us.

Remember, we need not reserve leadership for the workplace—the leadership techniques described here will serve leaders well in the home and all other places where interpersonal relationships govern a group's ability to meet its goals.

The leader is onstage; the leader is in a fishbowl—all are watching you, and you are influencing them.

From the author, Dr. Henrietta Ukwu, MD, FACP, FRAPS

About The ABCs of Leadership: Leadership Guiding Principles

Leadership is growing ever more critical in all aspects of life, as the modern world presents each of us with an array of problems that need solving. I hope that readers will recognize that the skills and attributes of effective leaders (and followers) are within reach for all of us. This simple recognition may encourage people to attain the core attributes, behaviors, and characteristics of leaders, allowing more of us to live lives of service, sacrifice, and success.

Leadership Guiding Principles features a chapter for each letter in the alphabet. Play on words makes it easy for learners to remember the attributes of effective leaders, while also guiding them to apply the techniques discussed in the real world.

Leadership Guiding Principles communicates enjoyably the values, ethics, and philosophy that underpin effective leaders' style and the behavior that leaders use to shape their environments.

Leadership Guiding Principles facilitates personal development and growth in a straightforward way, avoiding the unnecessary complications sometimes introduced by complex leadership training sessions and books. Throughout, it emphasizes the concept that everyone can become a leader.

Leadership Guiding Principles focuses on core leadership descriptors that individuals can use to become better leaders and followers. In homes, workplaces, and communities, these behaviors improve interpersonal relationships and the probability of achieving desired outcomes.

Leadership Guiding Principles has been used successfully by the author to build and acculturate teams, compel audiences during keynote speeches, and espouse her leadership style and vision in a manner that allows others to reach their goals.

Leadership Guiding Principles offers an easy to read, simple to apply guide and self-development tool that leaders can use to create high-performing, engaged, committed, and trust-based teams.

Leadership Guiding Principles uses vignettes to highlight real-life applications and inspiring quotes from well-known leaders to reinforce key concepts.

The higher you aspire and desire to achieve, the more you need leadership skills.

Acknowledgments:

The quotes in this book are from http://www.searchquotes.com, and the arts are from www.pixabay.com.

A

Attitude, Authenticity, Acknowledgment

Attitude

"Nothing can stop the man with the right attitude from achieving his goal;

Nothing on earth can help the man with the wrong attitude."

Thomas Jefferson

Attitude is the one thing in life that we can control, and the one thing we let everyone else control for us. We can choose to have a positive, energy-filled attitude—or a negative, energy-draining attitude. Successful, effective, and impactful leadership requires a healthy dose of positive attitude. Indeed, it is essential for keeping a team motivated. Ever been in a meeting or event with individuals who have a negative attitude? The energy is draining and discouraging. Leaders with negative attitudes do not attract followers, as people do not enjoy being around them. By contrast, leaders with positive attitudes foster productivity with their can-do approach, encouraging others through positive reinforcement. A positive attitude spurs teammates to assume responsibility and

1

enhances accountability, as it instills teamwork, common goals, and shared pride in outcomes.

How can one cultivate a positive attitude? Gratitude, which I call "great attitude," generates a positive attitude that inspires those around us and brings out the best in others. Leaders with positive attitudes **aspire** to higher heights and **inspire** their teams to make tangible differences. Leaders with positive attitudes turn "**adversity to advantage**" and approach situations with a "glass half-full" mindset. Great leaders are **amplifiers**! They leverage what is going well to achieve positive outcomes and make a lasting and transformational difference.

Authenticity: Leaders must discover themselves, allowing them to live the truth of themselves and their roles. Authentic leaders know the values and principles they stand for and live them. They are self-**aware**. Authenticity requires courage, humility, a can-do attitude, and a strong sense of **accountability.** A leader's authenticity drives their team to take on responsibilities and to aim and achieve higher. Authentic leaders can interpret information, constructively communicate even the toughest decisions, and convey a decision's value to their audience. They assess situations with realistic optimism and can communicate the silver lining of dark clouds. Authenticity is at the top of the list of characteristics that people admire in a leader.

Acknowledgment and **Appreciation:** These are crucial ingredients for and outputs from a positive attitude. Try starting the day happy, with a smile, and appreciating your blessings and acknowledging your gifts. Remember that your family and coworkers are gifts and blessings; view them positively and recognize their contributions. Achievements and accomplishments come from teamwork. No one truly succeeds alone. Advocate for and champion your team. Recognize and reward both your team as a whole and the individuals who make meaningful contributions.

Practical Tip: Leaders with positive attitudes become the sunshine that lights up the workplace and home. The next time someone asks "How are you?" at the start of the day, try replying **"Amazing!"** See what effect you have on others.

Anything that changes your value changes your **behavior.**

B

Behavior, Build, Business

Behavior can be considered one's approach to conducting oneself, including how one treats others, provides direction, executes tasks, implements plans, and motivates people. Behavior determines leadership ability, style, and effectiveness; leadership skills are the core behaviors that leaders exhibit. Because motivating people to execute *projects* and achieve results is central to leadership, leaders' behavior must be informed by a good dose of emotional and social intelligence. Behaviors at the core of effective leadership include speaking with charisma; communicating in a way that inspires others; respectfully considering other people; exhibiting sensitivity to diversity of thought, people, and cultures; and acting with the thoughtfulness and constancy that establishes credibility.

As emphasized throughout this book, establishing effective, transparent, and engaging communication and *partnership* with others is crucial to overall success. Most institutions and corporations evaluate leadership by measuring performance in two categories: (1) people leadership skills and behaviors and (2) project accomplishments, including the *processes* employed. This dual emphasis highlights the importance of both the "what" and the "how" of behaviors that lead to achievement. In short, a leader's behavior underlies how they show up in the world and how others describe them; in effect, a person's behavior shapes their *profile.*

Build: Leaders are builders. Using the right core behaviors, they build businesses, brands, organizations, communities, homes, broad-based relationships, and of course, teams, their pipelines of talent. Influential leaders' positive, can-do attitudes inspire their teams to engage and perform at a high level. These leaders drive excellence with positive reinforcement; an effective and respectful communication style and channels; a clear sense of direction, purpose, goals, and value-added; and compassion. They lead by example with integrity and ethics. This kind of behavior engenders trust and loyalty and boosts team morale and productivity, allowing teams to work together to build lasting achievements. Furthermore, leaders provide opportunities for team members to develop themselves and achieve their highest potential. As builders, leaders do the right things and leave situations better than they found them, including their teams' potential to succeed. In this way, leaders add immeasurable value to their environment, beyond simply achieving goals. Leaders build more leaders!

Business: Leaders focus on **business**, driving success. They are *bold*. They *benchmark* internal and external metrics to help their organizations continually improve and achieve excellence. Leaders take the time to gain knowledge and perform due diligence. They are not afraid to identify and remediate gaps, so that they and their teams can surpass the goals they have set. Leaders carry their teams along with them every step of the way, so that together they can achieve great things for the business.

Practical Tip: Be a role model for leadership behaviors: be prepared, punctual, present, pleasant, proactive, productive, and passionate! Note how the behavior of your team changes in response.

C

Character, Communication, Contribution

Leaders must first be of good character.

Character is the accumulation of one's values, beliefs, personality traits, and skills over time. One's character can be described as good or bad, strong or weak. Effective leaders have good, strong characters backed by ethical behavior, earning them a reputation for credibility and integrity. A leader's character underpins their organization's culture and capability. Leaders must exhibit the courage to lead, serve, sacrifice, be transparent, tell the truth, give others credit, and earn credibility. They must display compassion for other people, respecting differences and building relationships. To achieve results, they must master collaboration, effective stakeholder partnerships, getting things done, and cooperating with others. They must develop the competence that underpins a can-do attitude, infect those around them with their confidence, champion change, stamp out complacency, consistently pursue results, and foster a culture of continuous improvement and excellence. In addition, they must create a customer-focused culture that engages with stakeholders and partners as strategic resources. These leadership behaviors, performed consistently, create a leader's character.

Communication: Constructive, courteous, and effective communication through well-established channels and mechanisms is the hallmark of an effective leader. Listening is an important communication skill that is too-often neglected. Setting and managing expectations go a long way toward establishing credibility, making them essential communication skills as well. These skills are particularly necessary when leaders play the role of followers—which all good leaders must do at times. Leaders honor their commitments by seeing them through to completion, which requires ongoing communication with team members in a way that instills confidence and encourages delegation and empowerment. Often this means being accessible through many communication channels.

Contribution: Competence is key to contribution! High-performing teams guided by effective leaders create solutions, identify the opportunities in every challenge, and actively add value. A leader's passion for their work instills a sense of ownership and partnership within the team. Feeling they have "skin in the game," team members are committed to contributing to projects, leading to success. For a leader, meaningful contribution requires knowledge, hardwork, and due diligence.

Practical tip: Destructive "C" behaviors—complaining, criticizing, and condemning—are "moles" that demotivate teams, eating away at their foundations. Try replacing these behaviors with constructive "C" behaviors—creativity, collaboration, and commitment. These behaviors foster a productive environment and high levels of loyalty to a team's leader and purpose. Reflect on the results you get when you stick with the constructive "C" behaviors. And never forget to communicate!

"A dream does not become reality through magic; it takes sweat, determination, and hard work."

Colin Powell

D

Determination, Diversity, Decisiveness

"Real leaders are ordinary people with extraordinary determinations." -

John Seaman Garns

Determination: Great leaders display perseverance, determination, and resilience that reflect their belief in the cause they serve. A leader's values, principles, beliefs, and priorities anchor their determination. Determination helps a leader stay true to their vision and realize their goals. It allows a leader to turn adversity into advantage, find opportunities in challenges, and overcome monumental hurdles to reach the finish line. We see this spirit in great athletes, who display unwavering determination to surpass the performance of all those who have come before them. *Purpose, passion,* and *performance* drive determined leaders. Determination spurs **discipline** and **development**, which in turn lead to personal and professional growth. Indeed, leaders take great pride in learning and developing themselves. Whether a "born" or "learned" leader, every individual can become more effective if they are determined to learn and grow. Leaders are committed not only to developing themselves in this way, but also those around them.

Diversity: Effective leaders quickly realize the beauty and value of **diversity**, whether of thoughts, ideas, people, contributions, or opinions, and of the power of inclusion. Great leaders enable others to identify their unique strengths and achieve to their highest potential. One of my most outstanding contributions is the myriad of talented protégés who I have recruited and helped develop and grow over the years. They have gone on to become senior and executive leaders across my industry. I am also very proud of the many teams and students that my philosophical and technical teachings have positively influenced. Conversely, I gratefully acknowledge the many mentors and coaches who have helped shape my career and life. A leader recognizes the potential and diverse skills of those around them and is committed to developing other leaders at all levels.

Decisiveness: Leaders are decisive. They exercise good judgment by making timely and well-informed decisions. They do the right things, even when their decisions are unpopular or their solutions generate unpleasant outcomes. They make tough choices after weighing a decision's impacts and implications, and then they manage the outcomes and communicate about resulting changes. Many leaders fail because they are indecisive, always needing more information and becoming mired in "paralysis by analysis." Often, these leaders delay making decisions, fearing the outcomes, and thereby experience the very failure they feared. Growth and success in business require action. By being decisive, leaders can take a stand and allow their teams to progress. True accountability requires leaders to have the courage to "own" their decisions, thereby instilling trust and confidence in their teams. For these reasons, decisiveness is one of the most valuable characteristics of effective leadership.

Practical Tip: Think of a decision that you have been putting off. Take time to deliberate, but then make yourself take a stand and take action. What is the outcome?

E

Excellence, Engagement, Expertise

Excellence: Excellence is a habit with peaks and higher peaks; it has no cap. Yesterday's standards of excellence are not today's, and today's will not be tomorrow's. Achieving excellence requires **enthusiasm** and zeal for continuous improvement. It is inextricably linked to three other "E" habits: **efficiency, effectiveness,** and **expeditiousness**. **Efficiency**: According to management expert Peter Drucker, "Efficiency is doing things right." It is the tendency to work well, without wasting time, money, or resources. Efficiency comes with hardwork and regular practice, as only practice makes perfect. It entails developing one's precision, accuracy, and dexterity in a particular activity. Becoming efficient at your job increases your chances of succeeding at the task at hand. Every organization demands dexterous, efficient people who maximize throughput. **Effectiveness**: "Effectiveness is doing the right things," says Drucker. Success in the workplace requires effectiveness. For example, in clinical research, a product's efficacy is evaluated in controlled clinical trials, whereas its effectiveness is determined in real-world settings. When a pharmaceutical company undertakes corrective and preventive actions to remediate gaps and risks, the effectiveness of those actions is validated to ensure sustainable, systematic, and systemic solutions. Effectiveness is critical for ensuring the quality of our medicines, and it is just as important in ensuring the quality of every other facet of our lives. **Expeditiousness** incorporates the element of time. When we become continuously efficient, we gain time; quality reinforces speed, and outcomes are dependable and reliable.

Engagement: The secrets of building excellence lie in the habits of innovating constantly, staying in touch with customers, encouraging everyone in a company to contribute, and maintaining the integrity basic to leadership. Highly effective engagement drives these habits. Present, engaged leaders energize others to perform. Effective leaders are inspiring; they engage their teams, audiences, and colleagues to galvanize them to take action. Not surprisingly, industry highly values engagement; many organizations routinely track employee engagement scores. Indeed, management sometimes uses employee engagement as an indicator of performance and talent retention.

Expertise: Expertise acquired from training, knowledge, and **experience** lends a leader credibility, capability, and competence. Expertise can also be viewed as experience done well. To gain expertise, a leader must become an expert in the field of leadership and surround themself with experts as well. To guide their team, they must have powerful, authentic leadership knowledge and experience. The statement "knowledge is power" has become a cliché. However, leaders are expected to display abundant knowledge and experience. Great leaders use their expertise to **empower** their teams and delegate effectively.

Practical Tip: Take the time to learn, grow, and develop the expertise to foster excellence in all your activities. Jot down five concrete ideas for improving your expertise in the next week, month, and year.

F

Focus, Failure, Feedback, Fun

Focus: Focus is the discipline that distinguishes winners. Winners use focus to craft dreams into aspirations, aspirations into goals, and goals into action plans. Leaders are winners; therefore, leaders are planners. They follow through on their plans, staying focused on their visions, goals, and teams. Steve Jobs was famous for keeping Apple laser-focused, and every company could benefit from the same discipline. At the same time, leaders must maintain flexibility and be willing to pivot, adapt, and adopt innovations— that is, they must be open to shifting their focus when necessary.

Failure: Seasoned leaders know a thing or two about failure. There will be times when "Lady Luck" deserts us, when things just don't go as planned. Inevitably, even the most brilliant, successful leaders will falter. Being able to own our failures is a trait that engenders trust and demonstrates that failure is not something to be hidden or passed on to the next person in line. We should view failure as a stepping-stone to success. History is full of the stories of individuals who took a string of failures in stride and went on to achieve great success. Everyone falls at some point or other, but leaders refuse to stay down. Their falls and subsequent rises eventually lead to success and a wealth of invaluable knowledge from lessons learned. Leaders must also have the courage to allow their teams to fail and learn from failure, so that they too can innovate and rise stronger. Those who are resilient in the face of failure become the true champions in life. So never give up hope!

Feedback is a gift! We all need feedback to grow. Leaders need to receive feedback from their team—and give feedback to the team—for all to develop. If acted upon, feedback helps transform the workplace for the better. To continuously improve, everyone needs to review lessons learned from both successes and failures. In particular, leaders need to understand their blind spots, which I call leadership "trippers." I tell my team, "I can see your face, but I can't see my own, and you can see my face, but you can't see your own... Therefore, we rely on each other or the mirror to tell us what's on our face." We also can't see our own sides or backs; hence, the need for 360° feedback. Feedback must be complimentary and constructive to highlight strengths and areas for improvement. Unfortunately, many people receive even constructive feedback as though it is negative. On the contrary, constructive feedback builds character. Receive feedback as a gift and do good with it!

Fun: Let's have fun, celebrate, and make friends at work. Most of us spend the majority of our day there. We'd better enjoy what we do! Steve Jobs said, "The only way to do great work is to love what you do." So make sure you enjoy your work, and try to find the value in each day's work.

Practical Tip: Remember: all **work** and no play make us dull. So let's have fun as we work! Think of one way to make your workplace more fun today.

G

Goals, Gratitude, Giving

Goals are the desired endpoints of plans. Basketball player Larry Bird once remarked, "A winner is someone who recognizes his God-given talents, works his tail off to develop them into skills, and uses these skills to accomplish his goals." Setting goals, whether personal or organizational, is the first step toward accomplishing them. Before setting a goal, your vision of it needs to be very clear. However, the 21st century is the age of not just setting goals, but scoring them. And to score goals, there is no way except sweat and toil, focus and commitment. As Donald Rumsfeld once said, "Amidst all the clutter, beyond all the obstacles, aside from all the static, are the goals set. Put your head down, do the best job possible, let the flak pass, and work towards those goals." Goals must be SMART: **s**pecific and thought through, but also a **s**tretch, so we can aim for the sun and maybe reach the moon; **m**easurable so we can recognize when a goal is achieved; **a**chievable and **r**elevant, so goals are not just "pie in the sky"; and **t**ime-based, as time represents money and value. I say to my team, "The coffee gets cold and we can no longer drink it," so actions have to be timely. SMART goals drive leadership, responsibility, and accountability, allowing an organization to be purposeful. Make your goals SMART: follow up and follow through!

Gratitude: Leadership is about gratitude, or "great attitude." I leave this term on my office whiteboard as a constant reminder of its importance. Grateful people are generally humble, happy, and fulfilled. They find things to appreciate. They feel privileged and not entitled, and they are humbled by the opportunity to lead and honored to have a following. They treat the "chair" they occupy with deep respect and are therefore respectful and respectable themselves. When someone leads with gratitude, their team can see their authenticity and servitude and also the purpose of the journey. Grateful leaders are positive, optimistic, and joyful, and their infectious attitude energizes the team.

Giving: Leadership is about giving, so by necessity, leaders are generous. They are constantly sharing knowledge, information, experience, expertise, strategic and analytical thinking, vision, direction, ideas, time, talent, compliments, and credit. They give others a chance. This may mean giving the inexperienced recruit the opportunity to learn and grow. It may mean giving a more experienced colleague the benefit of the doubt. Generous leaders bestow on their teams the authority that goes with responsibility and they can therefore expect accountability. A leader's job is not easy. Leaders are in a fishbowl, serving as role models and exposed to the judgment of all and sundry. They must sometimes sacrifice to maintain behaviors worth emulating. They hold a lot in confidence and give of themselves to develop others. But this generosity allows leaders to generate an environment of sharing, inclusion, and openness, thus transforming their organizations.

Practical Tip: Be a great leader who exhibits generosity of spirit— be a leader with gravitas! Try thinking of one generous act you can do today.

HONESTY

H

Honesty, Hardwork, Humility

Honesty takes various forms: truthfulness, moral uprightness, sincerity, authenticity. "To make your children capable of honesty is the beginning of education," said art critic John Ruskin. We all know the saying "honesty is the best policy." Honesty is the bedrock of leadership. An honest person will always have a clear mind and be afraid of no one. They can hold their head high and walk with dignity in all situations. Dignity, power, courage, glory, and respect will all follow the honest leader. In the workplace, honesty is sometimes referred to as "managerial courage." Leaders who exhibit managerial courage communicate clearly and act decisively. There should be no compromise on honesty, for as an American proverb puts it, "Honesty is like an icicle: If once it melts, that is the end of it."

Hardwork: We must work hard and SMART. Hardwork is honest and directed at achieving results. It must answer the "So what?" question. Where is the value? Where is the "beef"? What is the return on investment? Otherwise, time and effort are wasted. Teams pride themselves on saying "We are working hard." But where are the results? For example, if a team reports that a 3-day offsite meeting was highly productive, I say, "Great! Where are the objective data?" Perhaps participant surveys can validate the value of such outings and justify their cost to the company. Leaders do not self-congratulate. Instead, they provide objective, indisputable evidence of the outcomes of their hardwork!

Humility: Leadership is about humility—generosity of heart and a willingness to admit mistakes, take feedback well, and right wrongs. Leaders demonstrate personal humility amidst success. Humble leaders are eager to give credit to others. The word 'I' finds little place in their speech, for they recognize the power in "us." To hone your leadership skills, apologize quickly when you are wrong. Make restitution when possible. Practice "service recoveries," converting dissatisfied colleagues and clients into loyal ones with the strength of your response. Demonstrate personal humility. Don't cover things up. Don't let personal pride get in the way of doing the right thing. Give credit to others. Don't badmouth and malign others behind their backs; speak about them as if they were present, and represent those who aren't there to speak for themselves. Don't disclose others' private information. Establish a track record of results. Get the right things done well. Make impactful things happen. Accomplish what you're hired to do. Deliver on time and within budget. Don't overpromise and underdeliver. Don't make excuses for not delivering. It is one thing to work with poor performers who recognize their gaps, but mediocre colleagues who are self-righteous, with inflated egos, are incorrigible, as they are not self-aware. Beware of any such moles on your team!

Practical Tip: Let's be honest. Leadership is hardwork, and humility matters. Take a moment to think about whether there are any recent wrongs that you can right at work.

I

Inspiration, Integrity, Information

Inspiration: Something or someone who motivates us to strive for the spectacular. It brings out the best in us. We often describe great leaders as inspirational. They inspire their followers to pour their hearts and souls into achievement. When we face hardships, inspiration gives us the momentum to turn the tide in our favor. Artist Nick Cave once remarked, "An artist's duty is rather to stay open-minded and in a state where he can receive information and inspiration. You always have to be ready for that little artistic epiphany." Having received many awards and much recognition for being an inspirational leader, I recognize how powerful a leader's words and actions can be. They can help the team see that all is not lost, bring the power of positivity to bear in good times and bad, translate the abstract into the tangible, and turn poor performers into stars by polishing "diamonds in the rough." As leaders, many opportunities exist for us to inspire others. Inspirational leaders also take the time to listen to their teams.

Integrity is the priceless possession of effective leaders. Leaders with integrity are **a**uthentic, **b**elievable, and **c**redible (ABC). As author C.S. Lewis wrote, "Integrity is doing the right thing when no one is watching." Vision and passion are undoubtedly important in a leader, but so is trustworthiness. To be inspired, team members must see a leader's integrity every day in their decisions and interactions with customers and employees. Overpromising and underachieving are pitfalls that can undermine leaders' credibility and integrity. When they happen repeatedly, a leader loses stakeholders' confidence and trust. Your pronouncements are as important as the direction you provide. Employees look up to an honest person who tries their best to do the right thing.

Information: No one argues with objectivity and data. "An individual without information cannot take responsibility. An individual who is given information cannot help but take responsibility," says Jan Carlzon, former CEO of Scandinavian

Airlines. We all know the saying "Knowledge is power." Leaders make concerted efforts to be informed in order to make sound decisions. They perform due diligence to obtain the information needed to strategize and chart future directions. Assuming and speculating are practices that undermine leaders' credibility. Leaders need compelling information to convince their audiences to follow them. As software developer Levit Nudi says, "Information in itself is not powerful; power lies at the very core of being informed and making use of it."

Practical Tip: Be an inspirational leader and a role model for integrity. Be intentional! Think about an important decision coming up in your life and identify what information you need to gather beforehand to make an informed choice.

J

Justice, Journey, Journal

Justice: Just leaders strive to make every decision a fair and square one. When making decisions and distributing favors, they treat everyone equally, without bias. They keep open minds and work hard to rid themselves of prejudices, stereotypes, and biases. Today, leaders encounter diversity of all types and must recognize talent in many forms. They must be discreet and discerning in their assessments and prepared to give people fair chances. Justice is particularly important during performance appraisals; to assess employees fairly, leaders must be objective and refrain from favoritism. They must be careful to communicate clearly and provide documentation to support assessments. Many organizations now have hotlines and ombudsman offices to protect whistleblowers and allow grievances if employees do not get fair hearings or chances. However, it is the leader's responsibility to remember that the moral arc of the universe bends at the elbow of justice.

Journey: Life is a journey that ideally takes leaders from good to great. A song is not a song until it is sung! A scientist who cannot convey the purpose of their research does the work no justice. Leaders must learn to tell the story of their journey: the beginning, the destination, and the peaks and valleys along the way. A journey is seldom linear, but hopefully the trajectory is in the right direction. The concept of a journey is forgiving. It encompasses lessons learned and continuous improvement and recognizes that yesterday's decisions, though right for the time, may not be right for today or tomorrow. Reflecting on our journey allows each of us to re-energize. It is a powerful exercise for any team, allowing team members to analyze their progress toward achieving a shared vision and ensuring continued learning and growth. When asked to share my leadership journey, I focus on self-awareness, values, opportunities, and blind spots. I discuss how I overcame challenges and experienced growth and how each hurdle I overcame broadened my success and leadership horizons.

Journal: Leaders frequently keep journals recording their actions, achievements, beauty points, challenges and challenges overcome, bold decisions, monuments, and icons. Journals are great memory aids. As the saying goes, "actions in January pale in magnitude by December!" I keep a journal of what I call "miracles du jour," or miracles of the day. Many astonishing miracles occur each day, but it is easy to overlook them without conscious, keen, and astute attention. Recognizing these everyday miracles helps me focus on the blessings in my life and lightens the burdens. Of course, many journals explicitly seek to enhance one's leadership potential, highlighting needed skills and exemplary leadership models. Similarly, many leadership courses and books (like this one) are available to facilitate continued growth.

Practical Tip: Self-effort and the **practical tips** you've learned along the way are the keys to your success. Why not try keeping your own "miracles du jour" journal for a week? How does it change your attitude?

K

Knowledge, Kindness, Keenness

Knowledge: "Great leaders gain knowledge" is the apt title of an article by business consultant Ken Blanchard. The first step toward gaining knowledge is to accept that we are ignorant. One who feels that he has gained sufficient knowledge ceases to learn. There is a distinct line between knowledge and information: A person who has information is not necessarily knowledgeable, and there is no age or subject limit on the amount of knowledge we can gain in our lives. If "knowledge is power," the application of knowledge is even more power! Leaders pursue knowledge of themselves and their teams, leadership areas, and environments. They use benchmarking to determine their competitive advantage in projects and business. They strive to establish efficient information and knowledge management systems, maximize corporate memory, and leverage institutional knowledge and experience. Leaders also surround themselves with knowledgeable and talented lieutenants, who can help execute the strategies they have developed.

Kindness: Leading with kindness, compassion, and politeness is a great motivator and morale booster. Team members need to know that their leader cares about them as people and relates to them. The generous spirit of great leaders further enhances kindness. I emphasize courtesy in my written and verbal communication to prepare recipients to be receptive to the information contained within. Constructive feedback can be delivered kindly, so the recipient knows your aim is to support their development and improve outcomes. Leaders who are confrontational, abrasive, rude, and insensitive do not go very far, because they swiftly alienate their teams. "The end result of kindness is that it draws people to you," says Anita Roddick, Founder & CEO of The Body Shop. Practice compassionate leadership!

Keenness is eagerness spiced with agility. It drives strategic thinking, analytical application, and an acute sense of discernment. We hear about leaders "with a keen eye"—these individuals can synthesize information with unusual sharpness. A leader's keenness and agility in understanding and responding to business situations increase their team's probability of success. Keenness allows a company to differentiate itself from the pack and gain a competitive advantage. Leaders who possess keenness have highly refined perspectives; they make good decisions that are based on knowledge, and they come out on top. Wikipedia defines business acumen as "keenness and quickness in understanding and dealing with a business situation in a manner that is likely to lead to a good outcome," highlighting the primacy of this attribute in successful leaders.

Practical Tip: Knowledge is power. When administered with keenness and kindness, it becomes even more impactful! Think about one area of your work or home life in which additional knowledge would be helpful. What can you do to attain that knowledge? And how can you apply that knowledge with kindness?

Leadership is the ability to influence. Others

L

Leadership, Learning, Loyalty

Leadership is the primary virtue that every leader possesses. It represents the ability to influence others and the capacity to translate vision into reality. A leader knows when to lead from the front or the back and is comfortable working with subordinates. Without effective leadership, a group of people cannot synchronize their efforts to produce the desired results. A leader bonds with team members as friends, helping them gel into a strong, cohesive unit. Effective leaders create more leaders; thus, we can measure a leader's impact by how many of their protégés have assumed leadership's mantle. Leaders who develop leaders become magnets for talent from inside and outside an organization, allowing that organization to retain a pool of talented individuals with diverse perspectives. All great leaders are also great **listeners**, and with their passion, sense of purpose, and accomplishment, their lives make for great stories and they leave a great **legacy**. Their stories are told and retold by all they inspire during their lives, and later, historians record their stories so that their contributions resonate long after they are gone.

Learning and leadership are indispensable for each other. To succeed in today's ever-changing, unpredictable world, leaders must be agile learners. They must understand the psyche of their subordinates to help them realize their potential. They must be receptive to learning what it takes to win in business and to lead other people. Playing the roles of coach and friend, leaders must be self-aware and open to feedback, understanding their own blind spots. When I deliver feedback to my team, I emphasize the bidirectional nature of this learning opportunity. I ask for my teammates' honest feedback, so they can help reveal my blind spots to me. That mutual vulnerability fosters trust and friendship, so that leader and follower can enable one another to learn about themselves and thus continually improve.

Loyalty: Leaders enjoy loyalty from their followers if they themselves are loyal to their teams and advocate for their needs.

One of a leader's most important functions is to create an environment in which trust and loyalty are expected. Loyalty is a two-way activity in which leaders gets what they give. Team members know when their leader supports and advocates for them. Leaders need to respect others in order to be respected. Respect is earned and not imposed by fear. Loyalty motivated by fear is not sustainable, whereas loyalty that stems from admiration and respect is enduring. Effective leaders display trust, respect, and loyalty, and their teams repay them with the same.

Practical Tip: Would you rate yourself as self-aware? Is your team loyal to you? If your team members held an election for leader, would they vote for you in a landslide? Do you know your business? These questions represent a simple leadership test. As a leader, have you received a 360° evaluation? If not, why not set one up?

M

Motivation, Mission, Morale

Motivation is our reason for doing things. Self-motivated, determined individuals understand that work is not just a place to earn a living but also a place to grow and learn while helping others do the same. Such individuals are not victims. They are victors! They act rather than react and thereby spend less time blaming and more time finding solutions. They become leaders by relying on results, trust, and a credible vision, rather than on titles or organizational authority. People naturally gravitate to them because they are optimistic and fundamentally happy, despite challenges and setbacks. These leaders can take calculated risks because they are motivated by growth rather than fear. They define their worth in terms of the alignment between their decisions and principles. Hence, they can make difficult, unpopular choices. Managers abound in the workplace. As leadership expert Warren Bennis, Ph.D., said in his book *Learning to Lead*, "Managers are people who do things right, and leaders are people who do the right thing." The shift from manager to leader is the shift from "know-how" to "know-why." To be effective, managers must learn to lead, as their workers need both vision and guidance to become genuinely motivated. In turn, leaders must manage the resources entrusted to them wisely.

Mission: Many companies, communities, and associations have mission statements: short written descriptions of their goals and philosophies that define what they are, why they exist, their reasons for being, and what they intend to accomplish. Basically, a mission statement captures an organization's purpose and helps it assess its success and direction. A mission is needed to carry out one's purpose!

Morale describes a person or group's state of spirit, as exhibited by their confidence, cheerfulness, discipline, and willingness to perform assigned tasks. It is vital that workplace morale is high and teams are engaged. Morale is usually high when communication is effective and direction is clear. When morale needs a boost, a leader can start by making the team feel appreciated. Introducing perks may lighten the workload and cheer up the team. When employees have positive feelings about their work environment and believe that they can meet their most important career and vocational needs, their morale is high.

Morality, the ethics or morals that we follow or ought to follow, is different from morale. It is sometimes difficult to follow the moral path, but staying true to this path is what decides man's dignity. Morality should be matched not only by words but also by thoughts and deeds. Morality drives ethics, decision-making, and justice. It is an essential attribute of leaders.

Practical Tip: Leaders model mission-driven behavior and engage their teams in activities that drive the mission forward! Think about what you can do this week to motivate and inspire your team to carry out its mission.

N

Networking, Name, Novel

Networking is how we stay connected! It means creating a portfolio of colleagues and personal contacts willing to provide support, feedback, insight, resources, and information. In an article in the *Harvard Business Review*, Herminia Ibarra and Mark Lee Hunter wrote that networking is "simultaneously one of the most self-evident and one of the most dreaded developmental challenges that aspiring leaders must address." I call this aspect of leadership "making friends before you need them." Leaders must create a 360° network of friends, one they can tap to socialize ideas and gain holistic insights into an idea's potential impact. In Japanese companies like mine, the value of "nemawashi," or "laying the groundwork," is paramount; it involves ensuring that the relevant network is aligned around a proposal before its "prime-time release." Networks are equally important at the individual level. I was once asked at a leadership session, "Who is on your personal Board of Directors?" Nurturing a network of connections is one of the most valuable attributes of successful leaders.

Name: There is power in the names of our roles: representative, champion, advocate, ambassador, leader. What is your title? What do you represent? How do you show up? What is your brand or profile? How do others describe you? What are you known for? How do people refer to you? How well do you live your role? What is your name—not your birth name, but the name others call you when you are not there? These questions can be scary to ponder. Leaders need honest feedback to understand their names. It is important to keep in mind that what we call things is powerful. We all know the cliché "If you call a dog a bad name…" Leaders must be cautious and deliberate in choosing the words they use to communicate plans and decisions and to describe colleagues and projects. Names are powerful, so be careful in using them!

Novel: To be novel is to be new, original, unusual, innovative. Leaders must be creative to navigate the ambiguity of changing times, people, and business conditions. They must become comfortable with new ways, novel approaches, and innovative solutions. In this COVID 19–transformed world, innovation and agile transformation are more important than ever; virtual interactions now define the workplace, and automation and digitization are imperative to operational efficiency. These changes represent an opportunity for creative leaders to challenge the old and the status quo. Of note, sharing leadership across a team can enhance its creativity. Using this approach, multiple team members fulfill critical leadership functions, solve problems collaboratively, and collectively assume the responsibility for team outcomes, leading to a strong sense of ownership and pride in results. In global teams, especially, shared leadership can leverage diversity to spur creativity. Similarly, rotating the leadership of global meetings increases the potential for novelty and is well received.

Practical Tip: What is your network, your circle of influence? What is the name that people call you? How do you show up as a leader? Answer these questions and enhance your leadership impact!

O

Ownership, Optimism, Openness

Ownership: Leaders promote a strong sense of responsibility, accountability, shared ownership, and pride in outcomes. To achieve a "skin in the game" attitude, a leader includes their team in developing and owning a vision and identifying the goals and actions needed to realize that vision. Teams are motivated by being included in developing the strategy. Transparency further enhances inclusion and a sense of ownership. When a leader gives their team the opportunity to discuss impacts and implications, team members become invested in making decisions and creating solutions. Encouraging team members to make their voices heard, to be the ambassadors or champions for ideas they believe in, increases their motivation and feelings of ownership. During my work leading globalization efforts, I have seen respect for the principles of inclusion and transparency singularly drive the success of teams' efforts. People like to be included and recognized for their leadership abilities. When this occurs, they feel a strong sense of ownership, which in turn drives accountability.

Optimism: Inspirational leaders are optimists who motivate their teams with positive energy and effective communication skills. As optimists, leaders create or find opportunities and focus on solutions. My team members know that discussing "opportunities" rather than "challenges" immediately switches their mindset toward developing solutions rather than complaining. Optimistic leaders help their teams see the half-full cup rather than the half-empty cup and highlight how each team member contributes to shared goals. They instill belief in the project. They help the team weather the storm of failures by keeping hope alive, encouraging members to quickly pivot to solutions and reminding them that, step by step, the team will achieve its goals. Optimistic leaders collaborate and prioritize partnership, inclusion, transparency, and information sharing. They use constructive language and recognize the power of words. One of my team members once said that I deliver even the "most negative feedback in a pleasant manner with a smile." I smiled and responded that this is because the feedback is "constructive!"

Openness is a critical attribute of successful leaders. Open leaders encourage diversity of thought, ideas, and contributions; they are willing to consider conclusions that differ from their own, and they promote healthy disagreement that enriches conversations and strategies. Openness is not an easy skill to acquire if one is not born with it. Doing so requires a conscious effort to ensure that all voices on the team are heard. Leaders may have to solicit this level of engagement, especially if team members are not used to this approach. To promote openness, leaders may want to consider making room for shared leadership within the team.

Practical Tip: Winston Churchill said, "The pessimist sees the difficulty in every opportunity. The optimist sees the opportunity in every difficulty." Optimism is a choice. Today, try choosing optimism whenever possible! How does it make you feel? How do the people around you respond?

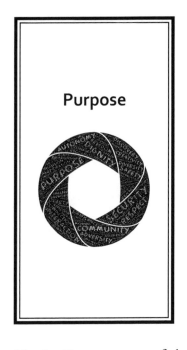

Purpose

P

Purpose, Passion, Performance

Purpose: *"The two most important days in your life are the day you are born and the day you find out why."* —*Mark Twain*. Purpose, one of the keys to successful leadership, is what motivates leaders. Successful people do not lose their sense of purpose! By keeping their purpose fixed, like the North Star, they serve as a compass for those around them. A leader's purpose emerges throughout their life; this thread woven throughout their personal journey fuels their legacy, shaping their values and determining what they stand for. A leadership retreat allowed me to articulate my purpose—to inspire and transform people with vision and passion—and realize how integral it is to who I am. In the business context, great leaders and high-performing companies have a clear answer to the question every employee asks: "Why are we doing this, and what is the value?" Purpose-driven leaders know where they want to take their organization and can articulate the actionable steps needed to get there. One's purpose is much bigger than their career or goals. It continues after a position or career is over. It is our brand, our calling, who we are. It is always inside us trying to express itself, though we sometimes unconsciously inhibit it. Many times I ask my teams for their "raison d'être," the reason why they exist. This helps us drill to the core of their roles and responsibilities and the value therein. **P**urpose, **p**assion, and **p**erformance are inextricably linked; purpose fuels passion and releases performance energy. As leadership expert Steve Moore states, "If vision is 'what you see' as a leader, passion makes what you see important." Vision without passion is mechanical. Vision with passion is inspirational—and it all stems from purpose.

Passion: If one thing differentiates the most effective leaders from their peers, it is their unwavering passion and perseverance, even in the face of overwhelming odds. Purpose fuels passion, and passion drives creativity and releases the energy needed for optimal performance. Effective leaders are passionate about their vision, which makes it compelling. Passion can be issue- or interest-based;

some leaders pursue social causes, and others are passionate about other specific issues. I am passionate about inspirational and transformative leadership!

Performance: By motivating and inspiring, leaders can influence the performance of their teams. I transform performance by enabling teams to translate their shared vision into the actions that will propel us forward on our journey. My current team has transformed to the extent that it is barely recognizable as the group that started the journey together; the way members convey information, accomplish initiatives, and achieve outcomes has improved dramatically. My analogy for this type of performance transformation is a metamorphosis. Just as when a caterpillar turns into a butterfly, no resemblance exists between the starting material and the outcome. A team can capture this transformation by mapping its journey toward achieving its vision.

Practical Tip: Instead of being a transactional leader, be a transformational one. Think about the people with whom you work. How can you motivate and inspire them to transform your team's performance?

Q

ality

"Quality is everyone's responsibility."

W. Edwards Deming

Quality, Qualified, Quintessence

Quality can be defined as a degree or standard of excellence, a distinctive attribute or characteristic possessed by someone or something, or a product's condition. All of these definitions are relevant to the discussion of quality's role in leadership. Leaders are responsible for the quality of their teams' performance and output, as well as the quality of their interactions with others. Effective leaders produce high-quality teams and outcomes. They set standards of excellence by providing their teams with the tools to assure a minimal threshold of excellence while also allowing for creativity. Effective leaders guide their teams to success by inspiring them to perform at their highest level and reach their full potential.

Qualified: Before we can be considered qualified to do a job, we must fulfill certain prerequisites. Continuous learning, experience, and expertise further enhance our qualifications. What are the qualifications for leadership? More often than not, we expect individuals to learn leadership on the job, through coaching opportunities, for example, after they have advanced to a leadership position. The qualifications for leadership are not about university degrees or previous titles. Yes, those things help, but your most important qualifications are how your life and experiences have prepared you to be exactly where you are now, making you the best person for your job. We don't get to pick how qualified we are. It's the culmination of thousands of individual decisions that have made us who and what we are.

Quintessence: The quintessence of leadership sits on the foundation of character. Quintessential leaders epitomize compassionate leadership, coming from a position of humility and self-control. They focus on collective input from their teams. They are invested in their teams and are committed to helping them develop and grow. They are team players and do not make the conversation about themselves by highlighting their own specific contributions or accomplishments. Quintessential leaders are confident enough to acknowledge that it is all about God, and they give their very best to God whether human eyes see it or not. There is something spiritual and pure about quintessential leaders. They have credible voices and stand up for what is right and equitable. They have the managerial courage to stand up for honesty, and they ensure their communication is transparent and robust. Quintessential leaders have high levels of integrity, and people seek them out for their trusted opinions. They embody the descriptions of leaders provided in this *ABCs of Leadership* book.

Practical Tip: Be a quintessential leader! Think about the attributes of leadership discussed in this book thus far. What are the five attributes that you most need to improve? What is a straightforward way that you could improve in each area?

R

Responsibility, Resilience, Reward

Responsibility: Leadership starts with understanding and taking responsibility. Responsibility is a privilege and honor, and the positive attitude that stems from this recognition will allow an individual to lead their team to positive outcomes. Leaders do not make excuses; they give credit for good results to the team and take responsibility for opportunities to improve. A leader's responsibility encompasses not just overseeing projects or portfolios, but also, as espoused earlier in this book, providing vision and direction, improving processes, enhancing partnerships, displaying behavior worth emulating, and developing their team. Indeed, nurturing a team's development and growing more leaders is a crucial responsibility of leaders. As Jack Welch, former CEO of General Electric, said, "When you were made a leader, you were not given a crown, you were given a responsibility to bring out the best in others." A responsible leader recognizes the expansiveness of their duties and executes them all. They command respect because they respect stakeholders and engage them accordingly; they strive to make just business decisions, achieve sustainable outcomes, and take care of their teams and workforces. Responsible leaders do not shirk. Instead, they are decisive in addressing their responsibilities.

Resilience is a necessary attribute of high-performing leaders. It allows them to turn adversity into advantage. With a positive mindset, they can weather stress with grace and help their teams prevail. Resilient leaders provide clear direction, along with the required dose of optimism for tackling difficult situations. They help their teams turn challenges into opportunities. Effective leaders maintain resilience by listening to themselves, understanding their actions, and consciously using their coping mechanisms. Because they have social intelligence, they can assess the impact of challenging situations and new responsibilities on their teams. This allows them to identify how to inspire their teams to take a new tack after setbacks. A keen sense of purpose, passion, and a positive attitude are the core ingredients that fuel a leader's resilience.

Reward: Acknowledgments of commendable work and compliments, whether with words or gifts, are highly appreciated in general and are very much so in the workplace. Rewarding team members for contributing, outperforming goals, or exceeding targets is a strong incentive for them to perform even better. Such morale-boosting practices foster a healthy and productive workplace, especially when rewards are equitable and fair. Each of us appreciates rewards, whether they take the form of money, certificates, or mementos that serve as a souvenir of commendable work. Paradoxically, by concentrating on the work at hand, rather than potential rewards, one is bound to be rewarded.

Practical tip: Be a purposeful, authentic, and resilient leader! Think about a challenge your team is experiencing right now. Brainstorm three ways you can turn adversity into advantage.

S

Service,
Success,
Song

Service: Leadership is about service. Successful leaders are humble servants. They do not allow themselves to get big-headed over accolades. Though they celebrate success, they see accomplishments as stepping-stones to the next set of achievements. Leaders ensure that each team member understands how their work serves the greater whole. I let my team know that each member functions as a building block essential for success. Helping team members recognize why what they do matters makes them commit to succeeding and enhances the enjoyment they receive from serving. This approach characterizes that of what I call the servant leader.

Success: Leaders achieve success! Much has been written about the fundamentals of achieving success and the traits of successful leaders. The attitudes and attributes described in this book define the characteristics of a successful leader. Simply put, a leader can clearly communicate a vision and inspire others to work together, learn together, and grow together to achieve impactful results. It should be noted that success without succession is selfish and should be considered a failure. Successful leaders breed more successful leaders; they become magnets for talent by creating room for new leaders to grow. Some individuals may view workplace conversations about "succession" as sensitive; effective and successful leaders do not. These conversations are necessary. A leader should prepare a path toward succession early, by enriching the team with able talent and cultivating members' leadership potential and skills. A successful leader owes their organization a sound succession plan.

Song: A song is not a song until it is sung! I frequently use this saying to convey the significance of communication in working together to achieve desired outcomes. No matter how well a leader constructs thoughts inside their mind, if they cannot deliver their ideas to the team in a compelling manner, the intended message will get lost. No matter how impactful results are, their value will be minimized if they are not communicated effectively. "A leader is both a singer and a songwriter," says management consultant Jim Crupi. Indeed, the lyrics and rhythm of what a leader says must resonate with the team's hearts and heads to be authentic and believable. We hear the cliché "sing from the same song sheet" as advice to promote harmony. Leaders drive synchrony and cohesiveness across their teams to impose organization even amidst chaos. This focus on song and synchronicity is linked to clarity, an essential attribute of influential leaders' communication style. Furthermore, many analogies compare the leader to a conductor and the team to a symphony, highlighting the need for leaders to surround themselves with the "right players" and provide them with inspired guidance. Meanwhile, each team member should "play well thy part" and strive for harmonious alignment.

Practical Tip: A song is not a song until it is sung! Think about the song at the forefront of your mind these days. Are you effectively conveying it to your coworkers? If not, how can you change your delivery to better resonate with their hearts and heads?

There is no "I" in TEAM

T

Team, Talent, Trust

Team: Without teams, leaders cannot succeed. They cannot execute their strategies effectively or achieve their visions. In building teams, they should seek out individuals who have demonstrated high performance, integrity, and the desire to assume greater levels of responsibility. For humble leaders, teams are the engine for success. These leaders develop team members and grant them the freedom to carry out tasks as they see fit. They create a safe environment for members to speak their minds. Effective leaders encourage cross-pollination of ideas among team members to build a culture of innovation and learning. Teamwork is necessary for any team of workers or players to succeed. It entails working together in sync to increase efficiency and maximize throughput. Each member of the team has a unique role to play and serves the team differently. When all members give their best in unison, synergy allows the team to accomplish its goals in a much shorter timeframe than would otherwise be possible. Indeed, effective leadership involves inspiring ordinary people to do superior work. Leaders must make sure the efforts of the entire team are visible and let the light shine on others. When the need arises, leaders roll up their sleeves and jump in the trenches with their teams, whether to teach them new skills or prepare them for a tough executive meeting. They help team members put their best foot forward to help them swim, instead of allowing them to sink. This approach fosters mutual loyalty between leader and team. I like to work with my team members to help them grow and transform; one of the highlights of leadership is the gratification that one feels when watching protégés advance to new heights.

Talent describes one's natural ability to do something. Now more than ever, recruiting and retaining great talent is a challenge. The rapid change that surrounds us requires high performers to be agile at learning on the fly. Developing and maintaining a robust talent pipeline is a critical success factor for organizations. Some leaders are known to be "magnets for talent," as their leadership style draws and retains talent.

Trust is required between a team and its leader: all members, but particularly the leader, must display credibility and integrity. Trust is bidirectional. Leaders must extend trust to those who extend trust to them. The only way to make people trustworthy is to trust them. As Jack Welch said, "Trust happens when leaders are transparent."

Practical Tip: Brainstorm five strategies you can use to recruit and retain great talent and establish trust based on your actions. These actions will allow you to build strong, high-performing teams and empower them.

*Unity is strength...
when there is
teamwork and
collaboration,
wonderful things be
achieved.*

U

Unity,
Universe,
Umpire

Unity: Leaders build and promote unity. They encourage team members to work, learn, and grow together, improving engagement, performance, and productivity. When a leader prioritizes transparency and effective communication, their team trusts them and thrives. Team members look for ways to contribute, knowing their efforts will be recognized. In promoting unity, a leader must focus on inclusiveness, equity, and bringing people together. They must help all members of the team understand how their work contributes to the big picture. When fostering unity, it is also helpful to identify team members' pet peeves and ensure that all members respect the team's rules of engagement. Positive behavior from the leader fosters positive behavior from the team. A healthy and harmonious work environment is crucial to achieving unity and hence success.

Universe: The "universe" represents the ecosystem within a leader's remit and reach. It is paramount that leaders understand their universe of responsibility, so they do not neglect areas of import. In assessing my leadership universe, I consider the five P's: people, projects or portfolios, process (which includes systems and technology/innovation), partnership, and profile. Analyzing each of these components of the leadership universe ensures a comprehensive understanding of one's responsibilities. When considering the people in one's universe, a leader should think beyond their immediate team to consider customers and stakeholders. Likewise, partnerships encompass crosscutting relationships both within and outside an organization. We should also take an expansive view of profile. A team's profile extends from its development of a vision to its achievement of that vision. We can assess a team's profile via internal and external surveys of how the team and its leaders are perceived and through external benchmarking to similar businesses. Using comprehensive assessments guided by the five P's, leaders can begin to appreciate the complexity of the universe for which they are responsible.

Umpire: Many analogies compare leaders to umpires. Effective leaders can also be described as coaches, as they must be able to clearly articulate a vision and use their passion to drive the team to achieve it. Both leaders and coaches have to be passionately committed to their purpose, but they must also know when to change direction and do so decisively. Resilience is the name of the game. Creating a healthy and productive work or play environment is crucial to a team's success. In today's world of increasingly virtual work, a need is growing for creative facetime and team-building opportunities. In addition, high-performance teams thrive where laughter, joy, and fun exist. Fun at work can help re-energize a team and foster engagement. Effective umpires, coaches, and leaders meld fun, fairness, passion, and commitment.

Practical Tip: Effective leaders promote a fair, unified, harmonious work environment. Think about how you, as an umpire, can facilitate such a setting for the people in your leadership universe.

V

Vision, Voice, Value

Vision and Visibility: Leaders have vision! And they, in turn, are visible. Vision is a leader's ability to see the destination, the end goal, or the transformed state before it is achieved. Leaders have to have a vision before they can create actionable plans to turn that vision into a reality, just as we need a destination before a GPS device can tell us where to go. A leader's success hinges on clearly communicating their vision to galvanize their team to take ownership of it. Leaders focus on vision, goals, and people; with their teams, they determine the goals and actions needed to achieve a vision and then take action on their plans. A vision without action is a dream. Action without vision is simply a way to pass the time. Action with vision, however, makes a positive difference. Vision is the very essence of a leader, the driving force behind their desire to gain influence. Simply put, leadership is the ability to inspire others to achieve shared objectives. Jeff Weiner, CEO of LinkedIn, says of the ability to inspire, "It starts with vision, and the clarity of vision that the leader has, and the ability to think about where they ultimately want to take the business, take the company, take the team, take a particular product." A compelling vision should be simple, succinct, and visual. It should provide a guidepost to a destination. It should answer the question "Where are we going?" Effective leaders create a vision, articulate the vision, passionately own the vision, and relentlessly drive it to completion. In this way, the vision becomes second nature to the entire team. Share your vision and work with your team to establish goals, outline strategies, and identify priorities to achieve it.

Voice is at the heart of a leader's power and presence. A credible, constructive, compelling voice is the hallmark of a leader. With such a voice, a leader can align their team around a vision and elicit excellence. A knowledgeable leader's voice also rings with compassion, courage, and equity. It becomes formidable, helping the leader gain their team's trust and loyalty.

Value: Leaders add value. When assessing any course of action, one should begin by asking the questions "Why?" and "So what?" When leaders bring these fundamental questions to the fore, it helps them and their teams prioritize, evaluate return on investment, and focus on the "need to have" vs. the "nice to have." A focus on value allows them to align their actions with an activity's purpose.

Practical Tip: The three "V's" of leadership are visibility, voice, and value. They are equipotent and inextricably linked. These attributes speak to the very presence of a leader. How would you rate your visibility, voice, and value? If improvement is needed, what concrete actions can you take?

W

Words,
Wisdom,
Work Ethic

Honest, hard work makes the difference.

Words are powerful. We can use many words to describe leaders' attributes, behaviors, and characters, as is evident from this book. This segment discusses how leaders can use constructive and courteous communication to be effective, build their teams, and establish credibility. Words have the power to break down or build up; they are tools of influence when used well and appropriately. It is words that allow a leader to rally their team to a clarion call. Words are the form taken by the voices we hear. Words are at the heart of a leader's influence and power. We expect an effective leader to have the courage to "call a spade a spade." Teams look up to leaders whose words resonate with honesty and integrity and who use their voices to unify the team around a shared vision, take responsibility, promote excellence,

89

and help team members rally after a fall. Effective leaders have a good dose of cultural sensitivity, allowing them to appreciate differences and use the right words in the right settings. They are humble and humane enough to frequently use humanity's three best words: please, thank you, and sorry. Leaders must use their words to support their teams, which means at times silencing their own voices to listen.

Wisdom-based leaders take the time to listen and understand issues before jumping into decisions. By making informed decisions, they lead with integrity. They are well respected as voices of reason. Wise leaders create more leaders. Because they are patient in building and transforming their teams, they can find diamonds in the rough—individuals who, with a little polishing, can enrich their teams and allow them to aspire to loftier goals. Wise leaders speak well of others and don't spend valuable time on frivolities. They recognize time is short. As I say to my team, "Time is the enemy." Therefore, discussions and actions should be well thought out, focusing on substance and adding value. Wise leaders stay above the fray and do not allow much noise or distraction into their workday. Wise leaders have the gift of discernment and give and seek out good counsel.

Work Ethic: Leaders with a good work ethic quickly establish their integrity within an organization, and the same goes for teams. Leaders with a good work ethic are knowledgeable about their projects and portfolios. They can clearly define their goals and objectives and are keen to follow through to achieve the desired outcomes. This focus on positive outcomes motivates their teams, who find their leaders' dedication and vision inspiring. Strong work ethics are infectious, and they improve a team's efficiency, creativity, performance, and productivity.

Practical Tip: Be careful what you say and how you say it, because words matter! Think of a sensitive conversation that you plan to have soon. How can you frame your words so that they build up rather than break down? How can you maximize clarity?

X

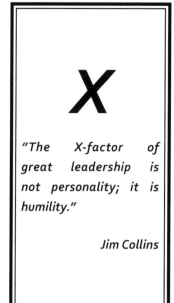

X-Factor, Xenial, Xyresic

X-factor: A leader's X-factor is what differentiates them from the herd. Many different X-factors exist. Some leaders are known for being team players and team builders. They are magnets for talent, create other leaders, and nurture a pipeline for succession. Other leaders are known for being high performers; their focus is on achieving objectives and goals. To accomplish this "what" (stellar results), they typically pay careful attention to the "how." This entails prioritizing clarity around goals, alignment around a shared purpose, and the team's health. Another crucial X-factor is a leader's ability to deal with ambiguity and display agility. Leaders with this type of X-factor bring order to complexity by creating simple, operational narratives that can be readily understood and embraced by their teams. This combination of simplifying and operationalizing represents an invaluable communication skill. Some of the best leaders strive to clarify their organizations' problems and then create simple plans of action to solve them. Still another X-factor is breadth of strategic thinking. Leaders with this factor help their teams recognize that their contributions serve the company at large, not just their specific units. Finally, there is the X-factor of executive presence. One of my CEOs highlighted this attribute when deciding whether to advance team members and when assessing incumbent leaders' performance. Leaders with executive presence can magnify and amplify their other leadership attributes to transform their teams and keep them working at their highest potential. Teams led by leaders with executive presence achieve beyond expectations. In short, any given leader's X-factor includes the extraordinary traits that they embody, as evidenced by their poise, behavior, body language, expressions, and how they show up in the world. With intentional attention, leaders can identify and enhance their X-factors.

Xenial: Humble leaders are friendly—or xenial—with all, extending hospitality to everyone they come across. They do not treat anyone with indifference. They do not let their elevated positions get in the way of making connections or even interacting with strangers. They are warm, approachable, and friendly. As a result, their teams are comfortable reaching out to them and inviting them to help resolve issues and conflicts. Humble leaders are not "weak." Instead, they are confident and self-assured enough to allow opinions other than their own. They have the inner courage to be vulnerable and accept their mistakes, and they have the strength to rise. Xenial leaders are generally lovely people and a joy to be around. They recognize that life extends beyond the job and that it is all about people.

Xyresic: Razor-sharp, astute, keen… These are xyresic attributes of leaders. Xyresic is not a commonly used word, but it is undoubtedly applicable to leadership.

Practical Tip: What is your leadership X-factor? Think of a few ways to enhance it or put it to good use in the coming week.

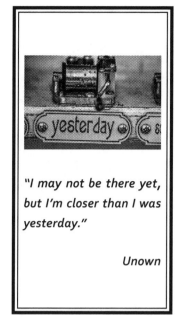

"*I may not be there yet, but I'm closer than I was yesterday.*"

Unown

Y

Yesterday, Youthful, Yearn

Yesterday: We are better today simply by having lived through yesterday! I say this quite often to my teams, to express the value of the experiences that we gain along the journey from yesterday to today and from today to tomorrow. The achievements, successes, mistakes, and failures of yesterday are great teachers. Yesterday's lessons strengthen our resolve and help set our compass for today and tomorrow. Great leaders are humble enough to admit their mistakes and apply the lessons they have learned to the future. They also learn from the successes and failures of leaders past.

Youthful: Humble leaders have the youthful energy to pursue organizational goals while taking people along with them. They also have the wit to laugh at themselves. There is a saying: "Stay green and growing rather than ripe and rotten." I choose to stay green and growing. Effective leaders keep learning. They sponge up new knowledge and experiences while sharing their own wealth of knowledge and experiences. In this way, they stay interesting and relevant. They keep ahead of changes, remain agile, and adapt to new ways of operating. They value creativity and challenge the status quo. As an example, today's world is transforming, by design and by default, into a digital environment. To lead the necessary transformation in their own organizations, leaders require a youthful attitude and the agility to learn. It is refreshing to encounter mature leaders who remain agile in responding to technological advances. They spearhead innovative changes in their units, sometimes even more rigorously than much younger team members. Great leaders are youthful in mind, spirit, and outlook.

Yearn: Great leaders have a deep, keen desire to excel and make a difference in the world. Therefore they keep learning. They analyze their personalities, relationships, careers, impacts, how they show up in the world, and what kind of leaders they want to become. Leaders must also have the openness and humility to learn from everyone and everything around them. I tell my teams that collectively we are like a great university, learning from each other by assimilation and cross-fertilization. Great leaders do not stagnate in the status quo; they elevate and enhance themselves through their deep yearning for information. They are like sponges, soaking up knowledge from many disciplines to augment their leadership skills and their teams' performance. A yearning for excellence accounts for the perseverance noted in most successful leaders.

Practical Tip: Stay youthful, stay green, stay agile! Think of something that you know little about now but find fascinating. Set aside time to learn about this topic.

Z

Zeal, Zone, Zenith

Zeal describes our enthusiasm or zest to do something. Zeal increases efficiency and fuels interest and passion. Successful leaders bring zeal to everything they do. This keeps them energized and focused and powers success. People show zeal when doing something they find exciting and worthwhile, like pursuing a new venture. Zeal drives one to give that extra bit at work, but it can fade away if a task is not successful. We often use the term "zeal" to describe the intensity of an individual's spiritual faith and confidence. Likewise, leaders usually have a palpable passion for and strong belief in their visions, which translates into zeal for their projects and products. Zeal and optimism are strongly linked. Together they account for the indefatigable energy that engaging leaders possess. Like many of the attributes of successful leaders, zeal is intentional and conscious. Bring zeal to your work to succeed!

Zone: What is your leadership zone? Many of my leadership visions and tag lines focus on excellence. I define excellence as my leadership zone because excellence has no cap—the drive for excellence propels us to higher and higher peaks! Leadership expert Bill Zipp describes three zones of leadership. In the Comfort Zone, a leader is safe and secure but runs the risk of being bored. In the Stretch Zone, a leader has a bold vision and goals; they are excited and a bit scared. In the Danger Zone, a leader's goals are overwhelming. Endless sprinting toward those goals leaves them physically exhausted. A leader must be discerning to determine which zone they and their team currently occupy. Many high-achieving leaders habitually occupy the Stretch Zone, but they sometimes run the risk of slipping into the Danger Zone. At times, I have found myself in the Danger Zone. During those episodes, my team and I were like chipmunks who bit off more than we could chew. We found ourselves continually sprinting until we decided to pivot to more effective and adequately resourced plans.

Effective leadership is a marathon and not a sprint. Guard against finding yourself in the Danger Zone!

Zenith: Achieving the zenith of one's leadership or professional career is a laudable aspiration. However, leaders often find that the zeniths in their lives keep changing—those of the past pale in magnitude to those just ahead. Therefore, leaders benefit from re-engineering themselves and their teams through continuous learning and development. Continuous learning promotes self-awareness, conscious and intentional self-transformation, and wisdom, allowing leaders to address both new and old blind spots. It's no coincidence that many leadership organizations use the term "zenith" to convey their high standards. Striving to reach the zenith of one's leadership potential can be transformational.

Practical Tip: Which leadership zone do you currently occupy? The Comfort Zone, the Stretch Zone, or the Danger Zone? If you are not in the Stretch Zone, decide what you will do to get there. If you are in the Stretch Zone, think about how you will ensure that you remain there.

About the Author

Henrietta N. Ukwu MD is a physician and pharmaceutical industry executive and a multi-award- winning inspirational leader known to transform the organizations and teams she has led and is currently leading. Very passionate about leadership and how everyone is a leader, Henrietta has in her first leadership book used the alphabets and words to share in an enjoyable manner the guiding principles of leadership. Henrietta has been in executive leadership positions over the past two decades in Pharmaceutical companies and knows first -hand the value of getting all to embrace leadership and drive excellence in outcomes as well as gain the gratification of work done well and life well lived. Henrietta expects this short, easy and fun to read book-The ABCs of leadership will find its way to all homes, offices, institutions, hospitals, communities for all teens and adults to experience the vibrance and joy of driving effective leadership.